390

2op

CW00806520

No..

Aut

Titl

-1.

-3.

-5

30.

21.

30p

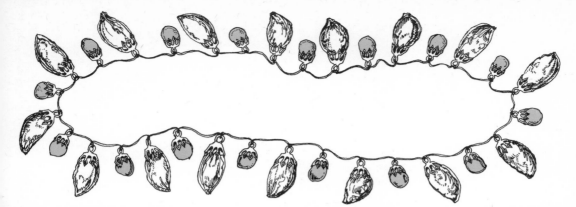

NATURE JEWELLERY

Janet Barber

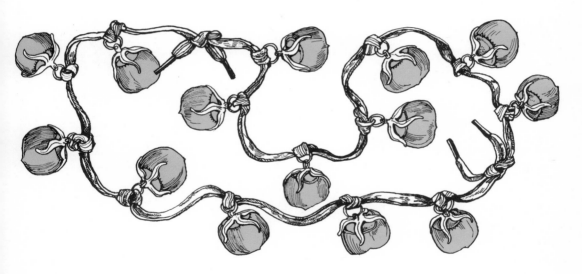

Illustrated by Elizabeth Haines

Photography by Gerald Hannibal

A Chatto Activity Book

Chatto & Windus

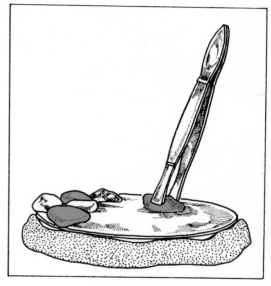

Published by Chatto & Windus Ltd.
40 William IV Street, London WC2N 4DF

Clarke, Irwin & Co. Ltd., Toronto

Other Chatto Activity Books
SHADOWS IN COLOUR
TABLETOP THEATRES
PRESSING FLOWERS AND LEAVES
FOLK TOYS AND HOW TO MAKE THEM
EASY SWEETMAKING

Text © Janet Barber 1975
Illustrations © Chatto & Windus 1975
Photographs © Gerald Hannibal 1975

ISBN 0 7011 5072 6
Printed in Great Britain by
T. & A. Constable Ltd., Edinburgh

To my sister Catherine

Contents

Introduction

When you think about it, jewellery has always been made out of natural things: stones found in the earth or picked up on a beach; precious mineral crystals like diamonds or rubies, gold and silver metals mined from rocks, or collected from river-bed deposits.

Wood, animal bones, shark's teeth, elephant tusks have all been used for ornament, ever since the days thousands of years ago when human beings lived in caves.

So, when you make you own necklaces and bracelets from objects you have found by the sea, or in the countryside and woods, you are only following the old ways.

The ideas given in this book are based on quite common natural objects you can usually find at the right time of year in the expected place in the fields or on the shore.

Next time you are in a wood, count the things you can use for jewellery: twigs; fir cones; leaves; wood bark; fallen branches; acorns and nuts, to name just a few. You may not even have to go further than your own garden to find some of these.

On the seashore, shells simply beg to be made into something to wear for decoration; so do pebbles and seagull feathers. Even the greengrocer and pet shop have some materials you could use. Think of walnut shells or sunflower seeds; they and many others are included in the following pages.

The only things to avoid are berries, which wither away. Especially, for safety reasons, leave poisonous berries alone.

Perhaps when you have tried your hand at making a few of the pieces in this book, you will be inspired with all sorts of ideas for making your own nature jewellery.

Janet Barber

A Few Safety Precautions

Jewellery-making involves tools and materials which can plainly be used in a right, safe way, or in a risky way. The ones suggested in this book are harmless when used properly, but please take care.

Keep to the simple tools we've suggested, and leave the electric-powered saws and drills to the grown-ups. It isn't necessary to use these for lightweight items like twigs and corks anyway . . . *so please, take no risks.*

Modern glue is wonderful material—it really does fix things firmly together. But be careful not to fix yourself at the same time, and to keep the glue off furniture and your clothes.

Some things, such as plastic resin, give off strong vapours. They are fine to use, and great fun, but it is *absolutely necessary* to follow directions for using them exactly.

★ If the packet says 'Inflammable vapour' make sure there are no lights, or fires or flames nearby.

★ If it says 'Wash your skin if any of this material touches it' make haste to do so, and where possible have well-fitting rubber gloves to work in. The same goes for turps., white spirit and paint-brush cleaners.

★ When you are outdoors collecting, especially when you are on the beach looking for shells, don't forget to keep an eye on the tide coming in, or you could be stranded surrounded by sea water.

★ Don't pull tempting-looking shells or pebbles out of cliffs, or other stones might dislodge and fall on you. Look for loose materials instead.

In general, take care of yourself !

Use and Care of Tools and Materials

The following simple tools and materials are needed for making the pieces of jewellery in this book:

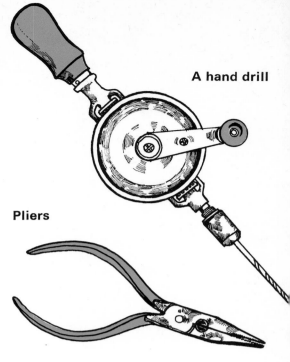

A hand drill

A mini-hacksaw

Pliers

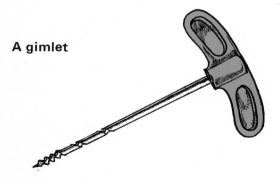

This saw is made of a thick bent steel rod, sometimes with a handle. The saw blade is replaceable. Use it with a piece of wood to protect the table when you are sawing, and do keep a spare blade by you.

Small pliers with rather narrow ends are needed for twisting wire or attaching jump rings to your jewellery in some cases. It is useful to have two pairs if possible. Special jewellery pliers, some with round ends and some with narrow flat ends, are now available in hardware shops as well as in rock shops and from jewellery tool suppliers.

A gimlet

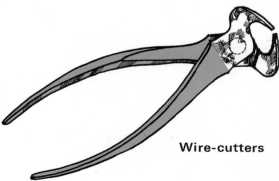

Wire-cutters

This is a pointed screw with a little handle, which you twist into cork or wood to make a hole.

A hand drill has a removable drill bit, so you can use different-sized bits and make larger or smaller holes if you wish.

A grown-up could perhaps help you use these. They are clippers, with a short strong cutting end for clipping firmly through a piece of wire gripped in the blades.

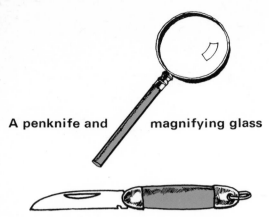

A penknife and **magnifying glass**

These are needed for stone-collecting so that you can look at the stone closely, and test how hard it is (see p. 42).

Sandpaper (also wet and dry silicon carbide paper for use with stones: see p. 43) Sandpaper in different grades is needed for smoothing wood and making stones or varnished nuts rough-ready for glueing.

Paint

Enamel paint in small tins, often used for painting bicycles, is ideal for painting jewellery. Use it with a small paint-brush and allow 24 hours for it to dry hard, before working on it. No varnish is needed.
Picture varnish is used with oil paint or for clear varnishing.

Turps. or white spirit are used for cleaning oil paint or enamel from brushes—white spirit is cheaper and less strong-smelling.

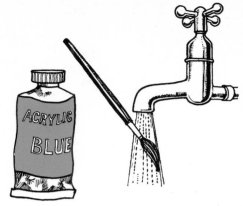

Acrylic paint is water-based, and you wash your brushes out with water after you have used it. Work quickly because it will go rock-hard when dry.

Special varnish for use with acrylic paint is available in art materials or craft shops.

A useful hint for keeping paint-brushes in good condition is not to dip them too deeply into the paint. If only the tip of the brush is used, all you need do to clean it is to dip it in turps. or white spirit (for oil-based paint) and squeeze the bristle-ends clean with paper tissue. When using *spray paint*, place the object to be sprayed on the centre of clean newspaper. Work outdoors or in a well-ventilated room, and do not place the aerosol can near a fire or flame.

Glue

Of the many kinds of glue on the market today, those suggested for use in this book are the all-purpose clear adhesives, such as UHU or DUROFIX or BOSTIK 1. They all come in a tube with a nozzle at the tip, which you can use as a spreader. Read the instructions carefully, because some—the 'contact adhesives'—have to be smeared over both surfaces being glued, and others only have to be smeared on one surface to be effective.

Two-part EPOXY RESIN is the strongest glue, and good for making jewellery. It has to be mixed in two equal parts of resin and hardener, before it works, and can sometimes be fiddly to use. Some kinds are fast-epoxy resins, and go rock hard in ten minutes. If you use this sort of glue, follow the directions extra carefully, and avoid getting any on yourself or your clothes.

Seeds, Nuts and Pips

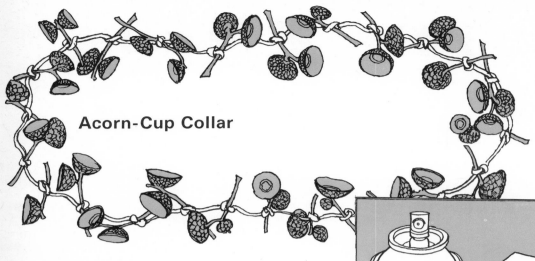

Acorn-Cup Collar

To make this pretty collar you will need lots of acorn cups with twigs attached. You can usually find them under an oak tree in the autumn. We used green string, but undyed or a different colour would be equally good.

Materials: acorn cups; string; gold paint (or another colour paint or varnish). **Tools, etc.**: scissors; a paint-brush if needed; newspaper.

▶1 Place the acorn cups on newspaper, and paint, varnish or spray them. Leave them to dry.

▶2 Place a piece of string on the table with an acorn–cup twig across it. Tie the string round the twig twice, close under the acorn cup.

▶3 Place the next acorn cup across the string a little further along, with the cup on the opposite side. Tie the string round this too.

▶4 Carry on like this all the way along. When you have nearly used up the first piece of string, if you want to make the collar longer, tie on some more.

▶5 To finish, join the string ends together in a strong knot.

8

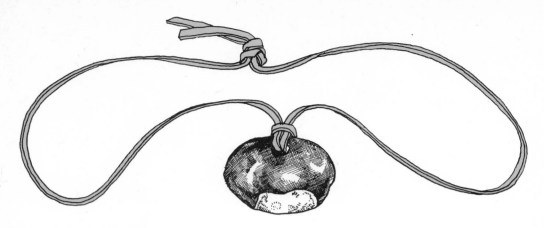

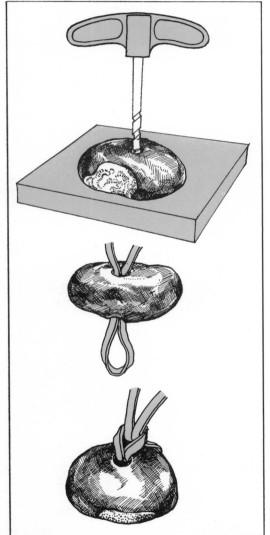

Conker Pendant

If you find a large, beautiful conker in the autumn under a horse chestnut tree, you could make it into this conker pendant.

Materials: a conker; a metre of leather thong (or you could use cord or plaited string). **Tools, etc.**: varnish; a paintbrush; scissors; a gimlet or metal skewer; Sellotape; a piece of board; newspaper.

▶1 First you will need to make a hole through the conker using a gimlet or metal skewer. Fasten the conker on to the piece of board with Sellotape, and also steady it with your hand while you bore the hole.
Press the gimlet point into the conker and turn it round and round like a screw, until it has gone all the way through.

▶2 Remove the Sellotape. Varnish the conker and leave it on clean paper to dry.

▶3 Fold the length of thong in two, and push the folded end through the conker hole.

▶4 Open out the thong loop and hold the ends of the thong close together. Put them under the loop and draw them right through until the loop is resting on top of the conker.

▶5 Try on the pendant for length, then tie the thong ends together and trim.

Bamboo and Cork Necklace

A piece of garden cane can be used to make this necklace. For the corks, perhaps you could ask the grown-ups to save you these from wine or other bottles. (Cork is from nature too; it comes from the bark of the cork tree.)

Materials: bamboo cane; 6 bottle corks; string. **Tools, etc.**: a mini-hacksaw; medium grade sandpaper; a gimlet or metal skewer; picture or other varnish, and a brush; a felt-tip pen and ruler; scissors; a bodkin; a large piece of board; newspaper.

▶1 Place the cane on the piece of board and mark it every 3 cm or 4 cm until you have about seventeen sections.

▶2 Hold the cane firmly in one hand, while you carefully saw through each of the marked places. Use only a mini-hacksaw for this job.

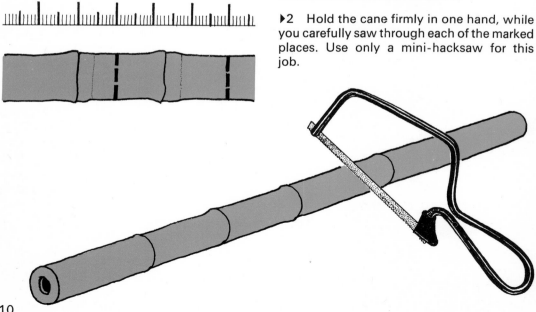

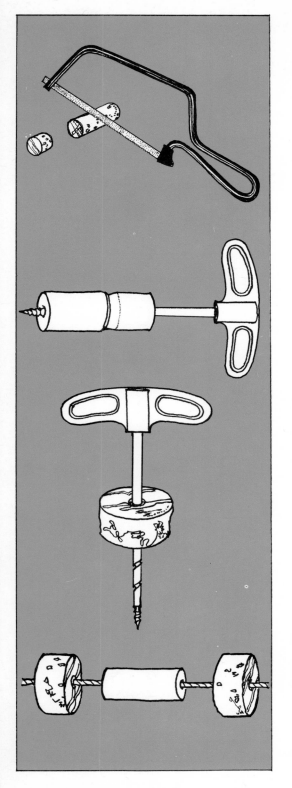

▶3 Saw each cork into three, so that you have eighteen rounds.

▶4 You may need to run the gimlet through the centre of any piece of bamboo with a joint in it, because these are usually closed across inside. As joints look attractive, it is good to keep one or two in spite of the extra work they give.

▶5 Rub sandpaper over the ends of each piece of bamboo.

▶6 Hold the bamboo pieces between your finger and thumb, and paint them all round with a thin coat of varnish. Leave the pieces to dry. Stand the brush in white spirit until you are ready to clean it.

▶7 Use the gimlet or metal skewer to make holes through the cork pieces, by pressing the point into the centres and twisting it round.

▶8 Cut about 100 cm of string and tie a large knot in one end. Thread the other end through the bodkin. Pass the string through the pieces of bamboo in turn with the corks. At the end, tie the string ends together.

Hazelnut Necklace

Hazelnuts are an especially pretty brown colour, and are made here into a long necklace. (It's strung on a pair of bootlaces!)

When you make it, you will be able to practise some important techniques, such as fixing on metal bell caps and jump rings, which are often used in jewellery-making.

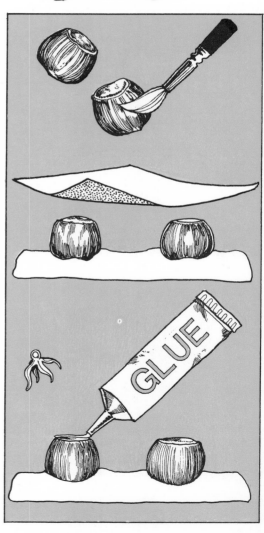

Materials: 14 hazelnuts; 14 large size bell caps (little metal hats with loops in the top) and 14 jump rings (metal rings used for hanging stones or other objects on a chain or cord); a pair of bootlaces or some cord or string. **Tools, etc.**: two pairs of small pliers; Plasticine; picture or other varnish, and a paint-brush; sandpaper; glue; newspaper.

▶1 Cover the table with newspaper, and lay out the materials and tools.

▶2 Varnish the hazelnuts and leave them to dry.

▶3 Roll out the Plasticine into a long sausage shape, then flatten it a little.

▶4 When dry, rub the blunt ends of the hazelnuts with sandpaper, to roughen the surface so the glue will stick better. Press the other ends in the Plasticine.

▶5 Following the directions on the packet spread some glue over the top of the first hazelnut and, if required, inside the first bell cap.

▶6 Press the bell cap on to the glued part of the hazelnut and push it down firmly so that the leaves spread out. Press the ends into the sides of the nut.

▶7 Repeat for all the other hazelnuts.

▶8 Leave the glued hazelnuts and bell caps to harden together completely. While you are waiting you could clear away the glue and get ready the jump rings and pliers.

▶9 *Putting in a jump ring*: This is a fiddly job that you might like a grown-up to help you with at first. It really is worth learning for yourself because you will often need to use jump rings when making jewellery.

Look closely at the jump ring. You can see it is wire twisted round in a ring, with a tiny opening where the wire ends meet. Now pick up both pairs of pliers.

(a) Hold one side of the ring in the pliers in your left hand, and the other side in the pliers in your right hand, with the little opening between them.

(b) Now twist the left-hand pliers towards you, and the right-hand pliers away from you, and open the ring a little.

(c) Holding the jump ring in one pair of pliers, slip it through the loop of one of the bell caps.

Take hold of the other side of the ring again with the second pair of pliers. Grip the ring very tightly.

(d) Twist the left-hand pliers away from you, and the right-hand pliers towards you, so that the wire ends meet again and close up the jump ring.

It's as simple as that.

▶10 Attach a jump ring to every hazelnut.

▶11 Tie the bootlaces together at one end. Thread half the nuts on one bootlace, and the rest on the other. To keep the nuts spaced apart, tie a single knot in the boot-lace string through each bell cap.

To finish, tie the other ends of the boot-laces together.

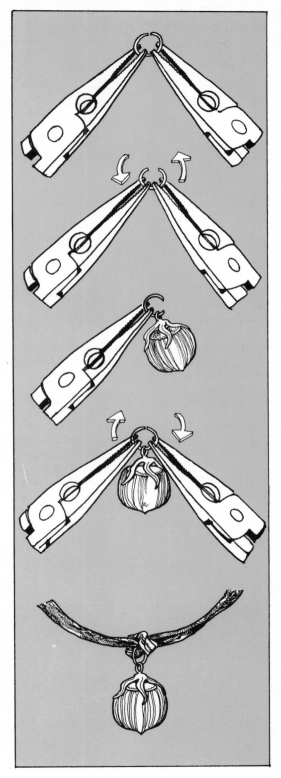

Acorn Necklace and Bracelet

If you can get there before the squirrels, you may find some shiny acorns where the acorn cups are, under the oak trees in October.

Materials: *Necklace*: 18 acorns; 18 small-size but flexible filigree bell caps; 70 cm picture-wire no. 2 gauge, or fine cord or string if preferred. *Bracelet*: 10 acorns; 10 bell caps; 30 cm picture-wire. **Tools, etc.**: glue; Plasticine; sandpaper; picture or other varnish and a paint-brush; Sellotape; wire-cutters; newspaper.

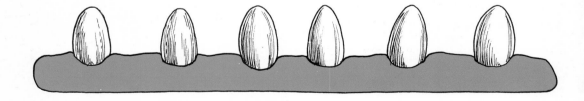

▶1 Spread out some newspaper. Varnish the acorns, then leave them to dry on the newspaper. Stand the paint-brush in white spirit.

▶2 Roll out the Plasticine. When the acorns are quite dry, roughen the narrow pointed ends with sandpaper.

▶3 Press the blunt ends of the acorns into the Plasticine.

▶4 Spread glue on to the first acorn and put a little inside the bell cap. Press the bell cap on top of the acorn. Do the same until every acorn has a little metal hat.

▶5 Ask a grown-up to help you cut a 70 cm length of picture–wire. Roll a little Sellotape round each end, to prevent the wire rope threads from fraying.

▶6 Tie a knot in the end of the wire, then push the other end through the first acorn bell cap, and draw the wire through. Tie another knot on the other side of the first acorn. Repeat this for all the acorns, placing them 2 cm to 3 cm apart and tying a knot between each one to prevent them from clustering together in one place.

▶7 Twist the wire ends together. Wind Sellotape over and over the joins to seal off the rough wire ends completely.

▶8 Make the bracelet in the same way as the necklace, but with the acorns closer together.

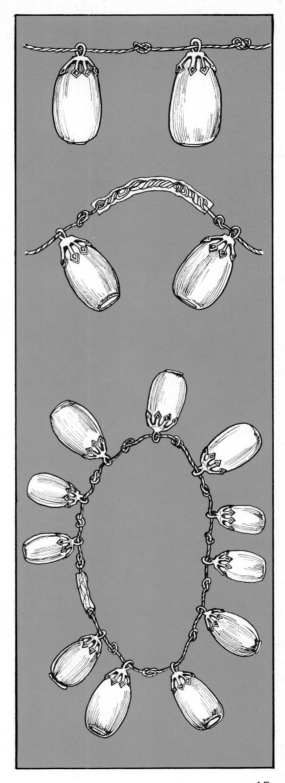

Cob-Nut Brooch

Cob nuts are a kind of large, long hazelnut. You won't have to look for many; only two for this pretty fob brooch. Or you could use any other kind of nut of suitable size.

Materials: 2 cob nuts; 2 large filigree leaf-design bell caps; a bought tie-pin about 3.5 cm long (from a rock or craft shop) or a large safety-pin; 20 cm leather thong; 15 cm picture-wire no. 2 gauge. **Tools, etc.**: glue; sandpaper; Plasticine; picture or other varnish and a paint-brush; newspaper.

▶1 Spread out newspaper. Varnish the cob nuts and put them aside to dry.

▶2 Roll out the Plasticine. When the cob nuts are dry, sandpaper the tops and stand them upright in the Plasticine.

▶3 Smear glue over the tops of the cob nuts and inside the bell caps.

▶4 Press a bell cap on to each nut and leave undisturbed until the glue sets.

▶5 Fold the picture-wire in half and place it under the bar of the tie-pin over the pin, so that the loop shows above at the back.

Take the two wire ends and push them under this loop. Draw the wires right through.

▶6 Now pull the wires downwards. Pass the first wire through the top of one of the bell caps, twist it up again and wind it around itself tightly. Do the same with the second wire and bell cap.

▶7 Place the two wires together at the top, and bind them round with the leather thong. Finish off with a neat bow or a knot.

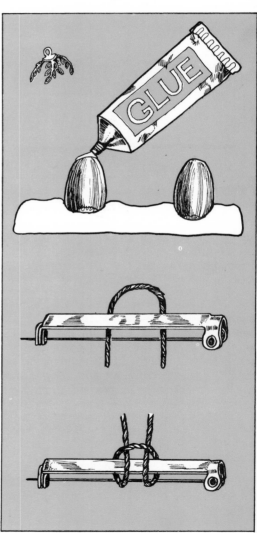

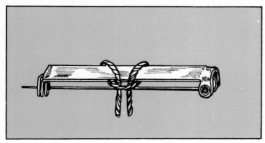

Oak-Apple Earrings

These smart earrings are made out of two oak-apples, each combined with a pair of acorn cups. Oak-apples are like little smooth round wooden balls. They are really the coverings of gall-fly grubs, and are found on oak trees; they make good earrings anyway.

Materials: 2 oak-apples; 2 pairs of acorn cups; 2 screw eyelets with rings attached; fine nylon picture-cord (from the hardware shop); gold paint. **Tools, etc.**: scissors; newspaper; paint-brush if needed.

▶1   Spread out newspaper and put the oak-apples and acorn cups in the centre. Spray or paint them gold all over, then leave to dry.

▶2   Twist an eyelet screw into the top of each oak-apple.

▶3   Cut two pieces of nylon cord, each about 20 cm long. Fold the first piece in half, then push the folded end through the ring in one of the eyelet screws.

▶4   Bring the nylon cord ends down and push them through the loop of the folded end, drawing them back until the loop tightens on the ring. Make a knot close to the ring.

▶5   Take the pair of acorn cups and place them between the cords. Tie the two cords together just above to hold the acorn cups in place. Make a third knot about 1 cm higher.
   Make a fourth knot right at the end of the cords, to give you a long loop to slip over your ear.

▶6   Tie the cord and acorn cups to the second oak-apple in the same way.

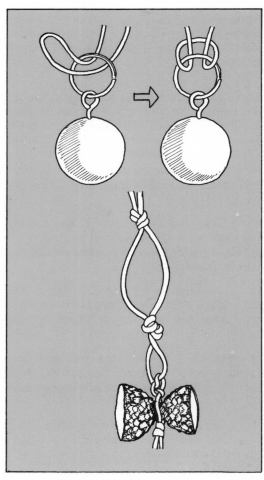

Melon Seed Pendant Bracelet

Nothing could be simpler than this melon seed pendant bracelet. If you string it on elastic thread you won't even need a clasp to fasten it.

Materials: dried honeydew melon seeds; fine nylon bead cord; a bolt ring and a jump ring (from the rock or craft shop); a bead. **Tools, etc.**; a medium fine sewing needle; scissors; an old baking tray; a sieve.

▶1   Scrape out all the seeds from a honeydew melon and wash them well under the tap.

▶2   Spread the seeds out on the baking tray and dry them slowly in a cool oven (at no. 1 or 2). You may need to ask for help with this.

▶3   Thread the needle with nylon bead cord and make a knot in the thread end. Leave a long tail to the knot, about 15 cm, to use for sewing on the bolt ring.

▶4   Pick up a melon seed and push the needle gently through the centre. Add another two seeds to the needle in the same way.

▶5   Gently push the needle through and draw the thread after it, until the knot rests against the first seed.

▶6   Pick up and thread through more melon seeds until you have a string of seeds about 18 cm to 20 cm long.
   Push all the melon seeds close together on the thread and tie a knot close to the last seed.

▶7   Thread the needle with the tail end of the cord and sew on the bolt ring clasp. Tie off the thread end.

▶8   Sew a jump ring to the other end and tie off the thread.

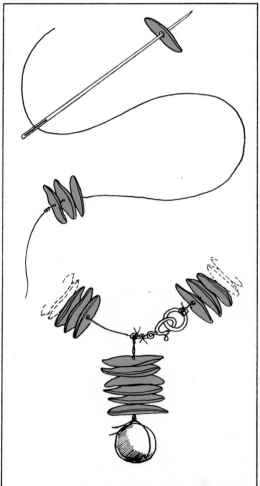

▶9   To make the pendant: pass the needle and thread through the bead, and tie the thread end round the bead. Push the needle through 6-7 melon seeds and tie them to the bolt ring clasp. Trim the thread end.

Seed Mosaic Badge

Seeds, pips and beans make pretty nature jewels. Think of striped sunflower seeds or speckled pink and black beans from inside green stick beans.

Here is a mosaic badge you can make from some seeds borrowed from the budgerigar's dinner.

Materials: sunflower seeds; melon seeds; sesame seeds; cardboard (from a cereal box); packaging Cellophane or special sticky-backed Cellophane called transparent contact adhesive; a safety-pin. **Tools, etc.**: glue; Sellotape; a ruler; felt-tip pen; scissors; newspaper.

▶1   Spread out newspaper. Draw and cut out a cardboard shape 6 cm wide × 4.5 cm deep.

▶2   Draw some diagonal lines on it for the bands of different seeds.

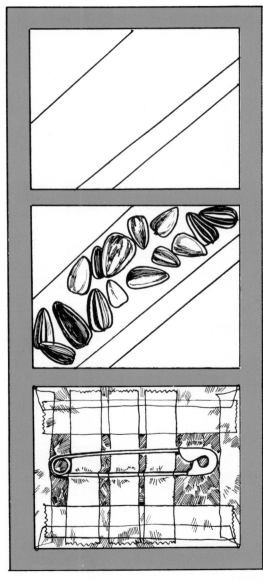

▶3   Spread glue over one of the bands. Place sunflower seeds on the glued area, and leave until the glue has dried.

▶4   Next spread glue over two more bands. Cover them with melon seeds. Leave to dry.

▶5   Spread glue over the remaining spaces and scatter sesame seed thickly on these parts.

▶6   When the card is covered with seeds and the glue is quite set, cut out Cellophane about 2 cm larger all round than the card. Cut off the corners and fold the Cellophane on to the back of the card. Stick it down with Sellotape.

▶7   Sellotape the safety-pin on to the card.

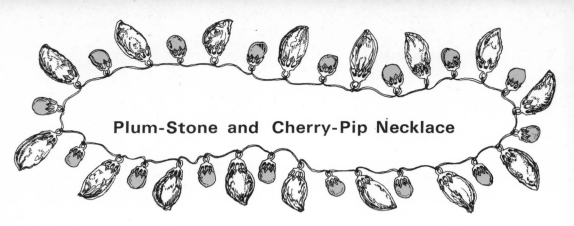

Plum-Stone and Cherry-Pip Necklace

You wouldn't imagine that plum stones or cherry pips or date stones could be made into delightful fancy necklaces. But they can be, as you will see here.

Materials: 16 plum stones; 16 cherry pips; 32 small, flexible filigree bell caps; nylon bead cord; silver and gold spray paint. **Tools, etc.**: glue; Plasticine; a medium sewing needle; scissors; newspaper.

▶1 When you have collected enough stones, tip them into a sieve and wash them thoroughly under a running tap.

▶2 Spread the stones on a baking tray and dry them out in a cool oven (at no. 1 or 2 setting).

▶3 Lay out newspaper and scatter the plum stones in the centre. Spray them silver and put aside to dry.

▶4 Place the cherry pips on clean newspaper and spray them gold. Leave to dry.

▶5 Roll out several pieces of Plasticine and flatten them slightly. Press in rows of plum stones and cherry pips.

▶6 Spread glue on top of a stone and inside a bell cap and press the cap on the stone. Repeat for all the pips and stones. Allow the glue to set.

▶7 Thread the needle with a 75 cm length of nylon bead cord and pass it through the first bell cap loop. Tie on securely. Thread and tie on plum stones and cherry pips in turn. At the end, tie the thread ends together.

Date-Stone Necklace

This date-stone necklace takes a little more time but if you make it well you will have a necklace that everyone will admire.

Materials: 16 date stones; 32 small (but large enough to fit well over the date stone ends) flexible filigree bell caps; 16 large jump rings; a small tin of blue enamel paint.
Tools, etc.: a paint-brush; glue; Plasticine; 2 pairs of small pliers; an old wire cake-rack; a baking tray; newspaper.

▶1   Clean the date stones and bake them dry in a cool oven (no. 1 or 2 setting).

▶2   Spread out newspaper and paint the date stones one at a time. Lean them against the rack to dry, for at least 24 hours.

▶3   Roll out and flatten the Plasticine and stand the date stones upright in it.

▶4   Spread glue on the top end of each date stone and inside the bell caps, and give every date stone a bell cap.

▶5   When the glue has set, stick bell caps to the other ends of all the date stones. This time you will have to hold each stone while you press its second cap in place.

▶6   When the glue has set hard, fasten jump rings between the date stones. Hold a jump ring between two pairs of pliers. Open it and slip it through the bell cap loops of two date stones, then close it again.

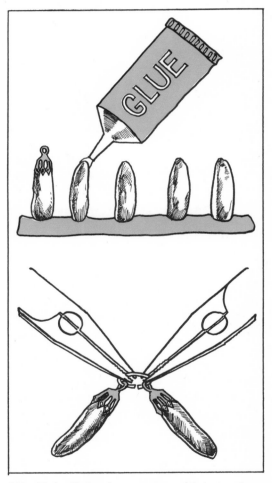

▶7   Link all the date stones with jump rings in turn, and at the end, join the first and last one together for a complete necklace.

Peanut Necklace and Bracelet

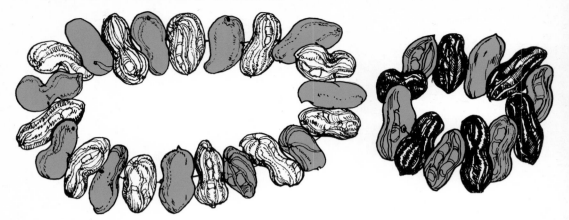

Peanuts are so comical-looking you can't imagine making fancy jewellery out of them, but why not make this zany painted peanut necklace and bracelet for fun?

Materials: 22 peanuts; two colours of enamel or acrylic paint (we used red and white); round hat-elastic or elastic thread. **Tools, etc.**: a fine bodkin with a blunt tip; two paint-brushes; white spirit; an old wire cake-rack; kitchen paper roll or tissues; newspaper.

▶1 Cover the table with newspaper, and divide the peanuts into two rows of eleven each.

▶2 Open the tin of white enamel paint. Pick up a peanut in a tissue held between your finger and thumb, and paint the nut. Lean the peanut on the wire rack, and move on to paint the next.

▶3 At the end, put your paint-brush in white spirit. Use the second brush and paint the rest of the peanuts red. Lean them on the other side of the rack to dry for 24 hours.

▶4 Then thread the bodkin with elastic and tie a knot in the end, leaving quite a long tail.

▶5 Very carefully push the bodkin through the centre of the peanut and draw the elastic through until the knot is reached. Thread first a red peanut, then a white one all the way along.

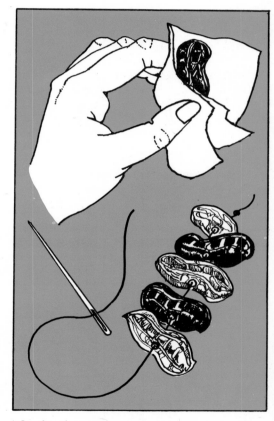

▶6 At the end, push the peanuts close together and tie and trim the elastic ends. A bracelet is made in the same way, but with only 12 peanuts. We painted ours blue and green.

Walnut-Shell Brooches

It isn't always easy to crack a nutshell without breaking it, but with great care you can usually manage to rescue half a walnut shell in one piece.

An amusing way of making jewellery out of walnut shells is to turn them into painted brooches; the humped shape makes especially good animals.

Materials: Several half walnut shells; several rounds of cork; safety-pins; enamel or acrylic paint in various colours; tiny shells for the frog's eyes; paper and string for the mouse ears and tail. **Tools, etc.**: nutcrackers; a mini-hacksaw and a piece of board; a brush for each paint colour; white spirit; Sellotape; glue; newspaper.

▶1 Spread out the newspaper. Saw the wine bottle cork into three over the board.

▶2 Spread some glue inside a half walnut shell and press a round of cork on to it. Allow the glue to set. Do the same with your other shells.

▶3 To make the brooches shown here, begin by painting the outsides of the shells with the main colour. Leave to dry for 24 hours. Put the brush in white spirit afterwards.

Ladybird: Paint the shell red. When quite dry, decorate the back with black spots and a black face, with a black line along the middle to show where the wings divide.

Mouse: Paint the shell white. Cut out and glue on two round paper ears. (Colour them pink or brown.) Glue on a string tail under the back of the shell. Paint some little black dot eyes and a nose at the pointed end.

Frog: Paint the shell green. When dry, paint on black rings with white spots inside. Glue two small round shells to each side of the narrow end for eyes; wait for the glue to set, then paint black spots on them.

Finish by attaching a safety-pin to the cork inside each shell brooch with a piece of Sellotape.

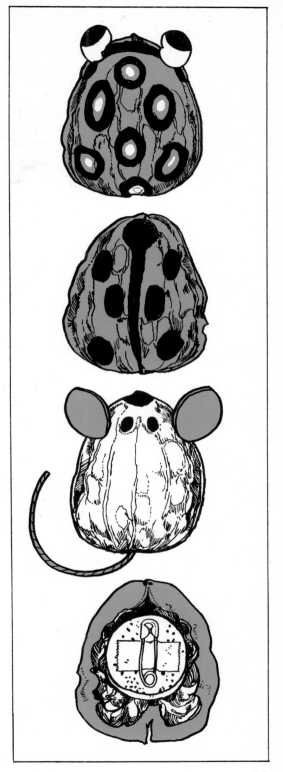

Woodland Jewellery

Twig Neck Ornament

Twigs can be pretty. The ones we used have got tiny decorative-looking knobs along the sides.

Here is a way of making twigs into exciting jewellery. This neck ornament is a ladder of gold-painted fir tree twigs, glued together and bound with leather thong. They could also be used in their natural colour with a coat of clear varnish.

The fir cones have been made into the brooch and belt on the opposite page.

▶2 Mark off the lengths of the horizontal twigs and saw through them. The thick twig across the top is about 14 cm long. You will need seven more thin and thick ones, gradually going down in size from 13 cm to 7 cm.

▶3 On a clean sheet of newspaper place the two thick upright twigs 4 cm apart, and fasten them down with Sellotape, to keep them in position. Arrange the shorter-length twigs in a ladder down the main twigs, starting with the widest at the top.

Where each twig crosses the main posts, dab some glue, and press into position. Cover the arrangement with newspaper, and place a heavy book or object on top.

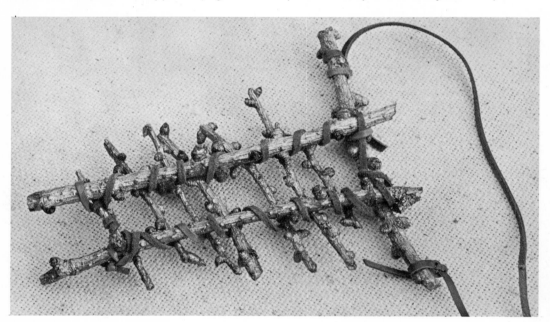

Materials: an assortment of twigs; 2 metres of leather thong; gold spray paint (or varnish and a paint-brush). **Tools, etc.**: a mini-hacksaw and a piece of board; glue; chalk and ruler; Sellotape; newspaper.

▶1 Spread out newspapers and the twigs on them. Choose one fairly thick twig for the two vertical posts of the ornament. Mark two lengths each about 18 cm long and saw them off, over the board.

▶4 When the glue has set, take away the Sellotape. Spray the twigs gold, or varnish them. Leave to dry.

▶5 Lace the leather thong from the top left down, winding it round to tie each cross-twig to the post for extra strength. At the bottom, take the thong across and up on the right side. Tie the thong ends together where they meet.

▶6 Tie a leather thong halter to fit you at each end of the top cross-twig, as shown.

Fir-Cone Brooch

It is hard to believe that these beautiful rose-like objects have just been picked from a fallen twig and sprayed gold. Fir cones are nature jewellery in themselves, and need no more than a mount and pin to turn them into a perfect brooch.

Materials: 4 tiny fir cones; card; a safety-pin; gold spray paint. **Tools, etc.**: scissors; Sellotape; a ruler and pencil; glue; news-paper.
▶1 Spread out newspaper and place the fir cones on it. Spray them gold and leave them to dry.

▶2 Draw and cut out a 4.5 cm square of cardboard.

▶3 Spread glue thickly on the card, and on the fir cone stub ends.

▶4 Press the fir cones on to the card. Hold all four in place with the flat of your hand until the glue begins to set.

▶5 When the glue is dry and hard, fasten a safety-pin on the card back with Sellotape.

Fir-Cone Tie Belt

Here is another simple way of making something pretty to wear using fir cones.

Materials: 2 small fir cones. 2 filigree leaf design large bell caps; 2 large jump rings; 2 metres leather thong; silver spray paint. **Tools, etc.**: 2 pairs of pliers; glue; scissors; newspaper.
▶1 Spread out the newspaper and spray the fir cones silver. Leave to dry.

▶2 Spread some glue over the stub ends of the fir cones and inside the bell caps. Press the bell caps on to the fir cones.

▶3 Use your pliers and fasten a jump ring through each bell cap.

▶4 Tie the ends of the leather thong through the jump rings on the fir cones.

Beech-Mast Brooch

Little whiskered beech masts open out like flowers. You will find them in the late autumn lying on the ground under beech trees. If you collect some with twigs attached, you can make them into this brooch. It is a way of using strong catkins too, but these should hang down.

Materials: 3 beech masts with twigs; 2 twigs each 6 cm long; a piece of stiff card from a cereal box 6 cm wide × 1.5 cm long; gold spray paint; a brooch pin from a rock or craft shop or a strong safety-pin and Sellotape. **Tools, etc.:** glue; a ruler and pencil; scissors; newspaper.

▶1 Draw and cut out the card shape to the measurements given above. Fasten the three beech-mast twigs to it with Sellotape.

▶2 Spread a thick layer of glue over the front of the card, on top of the Sellotape and beech-mast twigs. Press the two 6 cm long twigs on to the glued card crosswise, and hold them in place until the glue begins to harden slightly. After this, it should be set enough to hold the twigs without your help.

▶3 Place the brooch on a sheet of newspaper and spray it with gold paint thickly until the twigs and beech masts and cardboard are all covered.

▶4 When the brooch is dry, turn it over. Glue the brooch pin to the card, or fasten the safety-pin in place with Sellotape.

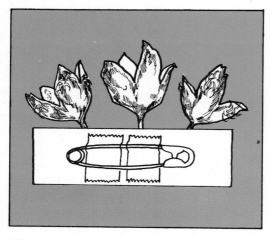

Ivy Leaf Badge

There are so many beautifully shaped leaves around, it seems a pity not to make some into jewellery.

Try this simple way of making a badge out of an ivy or oak leaf. (If you have found a brightly coloured autumn leaf you like, don't paint it. The colour may fade but it will be lovely while it lasts.)

Materials: an ivy leaf or any other leaf with an interesting shape; Sellotape; thin card or thick paper; picture-wire no. 2 gauge; silver paint (or gold paint, coloured enamel or varnish); a safety-pin. **Tools, etc.**: scissors; a paint-brush if needed; wire-cutters; newspaper.

▶1 Spray the ivy leaf silver and leave it to dry.

▶2 Place the ivy leaf on the thick paper or thin card, front side up.

▶3 Stick Sellotape strips over the leaf to fasten it to the card, as well as to give it a transparent covering.

▶4 Cut round the leaf carefully, leaving an edge of card showing if you wish. Cut off the stalk.

▶5 Take a piece of picture-wire 30 cm long and double it in half.

▶6 Twist it from the folded end to form a wire rope, about 5 cm long.

▶7 Take the wire ends and twist them together to join them. Wind Sellotape round the twisted part. Open out the loop as shown.

▶8 Attach the loop with Sellotape to the card at the back of the leaf.

▶9 Sellotape a safety-pin inside the loop.

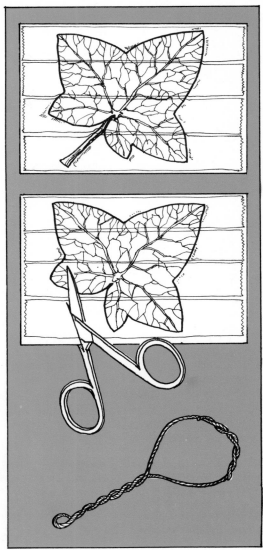

Wood and Thong Disc Pendant

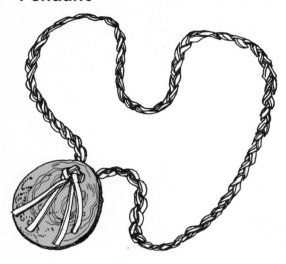

▶4 Cut the thong into three equal lengths. Tie them together at one end. Plait them neatly to within about 15 cm of the end.

▶5 Undo the first knot. Push all the thong ends through the disc hole. Tie a knot with two of them around the others to form a leather tassel, then push the two ends through to the back of the disc, and tie off. Trim the tassel and knot ends.

Perhaps someone will kindly help you to saw a round from a fallen branch found in a wood or a garden. You need a piece about 5 cm to 7 cm across and about 0.5 cm to 1 cm thick. At the same time, maybe you can get help with drilling a hole through the disc. If you do the job yourself, use a hand drill or a gimlet, and make the hole about 1 cm wide, by drilling small holes round in a circle and poking out the wood inside. Then you can make this exciting wood and leather pendant.

Materials: wood disc; 3 metres of leather thong (or string, or 1 metre of cord). **Tools, etc.**: sandpaper; brown shoe polish; varnish and a brush; a clean rag; a hand drill or gimlet if needed; scissors; newspaper.

▶1 Spread out newspaper. Rub the disc with sandpaper to smooth it on both sides, as well as round the inside of the hole.

▶2 Rub shoe polish on a rag thinly and evenly over the wood to stain and darken it. Polish with a clean rag, front and back.

▶3 Varnish the disc, first on one side, and when dry, on the other.

Wood Bark Wristband

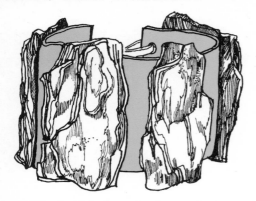

Wood bark picked up in the garden, wood or forest can be used for this wristband. If you have to prise off the wood bark, look for a fallen log or a tree-stump. Bark is usually easier to peel off from dead wood, but dry it thoroughly before you use it.

Materials: wood bark about 5 cm deep; a strip of leather or felt 16 cm wide × 5 cm deep (or long enough to fit round your wrist); 1 metre leather thong or cord.
Tools, etc.: glue; mini-hacksaw and board; eyelet pliers; scissors; a ruler; chalk; newspaper.

▶1 Spread out newspaper. Use chalk to draw a rectangle on the leather or felt 16 cm × 5 cm (or to the width of your wrist). Cut out the shape.

▶2 Punch 3 holes down each of the short sides using the eyelet pliers.

▶3 Using the mini-hacksaw and board, trim the wood bark to 5 cm deep. (You can mark the size on the bark back with chalk.)

▶4 Spread glue thickly on the back of the bark pieces. Press them on to the wristband, but not over the punched holes.

Put newspaper on top, and a heavy book, to press the bark in place. Leave to dry.

▶5 When the glue is hard, remove the weights. Lace the thong through the holes starting from the top. Trim and tie in a bow at the lower end.

Fur, Feathers and Bones

Sheep's Wool Lapel Pin

If you have ever been in wild mountains or moorland where there are sheep, you will have seen pieces of wool entangled in the brambles or bracken, or in branches of trees hanging over a stream.

Collect these scraps of wool on your next visit, and take them home and wash them, and you will soon have enough to make this wool badge.

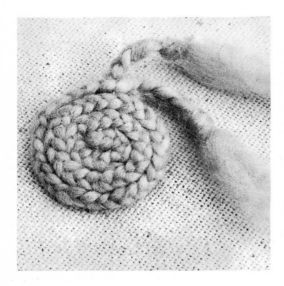

Materials: sheep's wool; cardboard; felt; a brooch from the rock or craft shop, or a safety-pin. **Tools, etc.**: scissors; glue; Sellotape; a needle and thread; stiff cardboard to comb the wool.

▶1 Wash and rinse the wool thoroughly. Dry it and comb it through with the edge of the cardboard.

▶2 Pull the wool out and divide it into three lots.

▶3 Twirl and twist the first lot together round and round to form a thin rope. Do this with the other lots in turn.

▶4 Match the three strands together at one end and tie them in a knot, leaving a 12 cm long tail.

▶5 Plait the three strands tightly and carefully.

▶6 About 12 cm from the other end, tie a knot.

▶7 Spread out newspaper. Lay the wool rope on it with tassels top and bottom.

▶8 Coil the wool round and round, starting with the centre about 5 cm above the knot of the lower tassel.

▶9 When the whorl is completed match the second tassel beside the first. Hold the coil in place with Sellotape across the front.

▶10 Thread the needle and knot the thread end. Turn the coil over and oversew the plait together round the whorls.

▶11 Cut card and felt circles to fit inside the back of the badge. Glue on the felt, then the cardboard.

▶12 Glue on the brooch fastening, or Sellotape the safety-pin to the card. Remove the Sellotape from the front of the brooch.

Bird Stone Brooch

Here is an amusing bird brooch with a little feather tail you might like to wear yourself. Or you could make others for presents, with different bird or flower designs.

Materials: a small, flat round pebble (about 3 cm across), either polished, varnished or plain; black paint or ink; a small feather; a round brooch fastening from a rock or craft shop. **Tools, etc.:** varnish if required; a paint-brush; a small round painting-brush to use with the ink; sand-paper; glue; newspaper.

▶1 Polish or varnish the stone if necessary.

▶2 Paint two black dot eyes and a triangle for the beak.

▶3 Sandpaper the back of the pebble to roughen it for the glue.

▶4 Dab some glue on one side of the back and press the quill on to it, so that the feather sticks out from behind.

▶5 Glue on the brooch fastening. Hold until the glue sets a little, then leave to dry.

Feather and Stone Lapel Brooch

This feather and stone lapel pin would make a lovely present for a grown-up. You could find two or three seagull feathers from the beach, or some bird feathers from the garden or country. Look out for some small fluffy ones for the front of the brooch.

Materials: some feathers; a polished, pretty stone; a tie-pin from a rock or craft shop. **Tools, etc.**: scissors; thread; glue; sandpaper; newspaper.

▶1   Spread out the newspaper. Arrange the feathers as shown in the picture, and bind them together with thread. Tie the ends.

▶2   Sandpaper the back of the stone, then glue the quills on to it. Trim the quill ends below the stone.

▶3   Press the stone and quills tightly together until the glue begins to set.

▶4   When dry, turn the spray over and glue on the tie-pin. Hold the pin firmly against the quills until the glue begins to harden. Leave to dry.

Bones Pendant

Bones or animal teeth make interesting shapes; indeed, they were often used in primitive jewellery. These painted chicken bones were saved at home. If you pick some up in the field, try not to handle them until they have been soaked in a bucket of disinfectant.

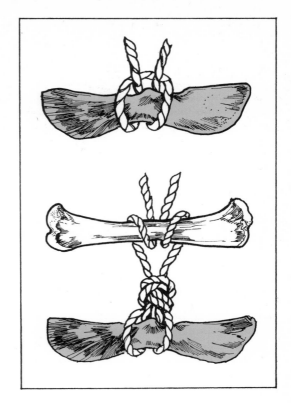

Materials: chicken bones; 125 cm narrow white piping cord (or thick string); red and yellow paint (enamel or acrylic); varnish for the acrylic paint. **Tools, etc.**: 2 paint-brushes; scissors; newspaper.

▶1 Wash and dry the bones.

▶2 Spread out newspaper. Divide the bones into the ones to be painted red, and the others to be painted yellow.

▶3 Paint the red bones first; next the yellow. Keep them apart and leave to dry for 24 hours (less for acrylic paint).

▶4 Varnish acrylic painted bones.

▶5 When perfectly dry, arrange the bones in order, mixing colours.

▶6 Double the piping cord. Place the first bone on top of the loop.

▶7 Take the cord ends over the bone through the loop. Draw them tight so that the loop is against the bone.

▶8 Tie a knot close to the bone. Place the next bone on top of the cord.

▶9 Wind the two cords over the bone and take the cord ends through the middle and up at the back. Tie a knot close to the bone.
  Do the same with all the bones. Tie the cord ends in a knot to form a pendant.

Seaside Jewellery

Mussel-Shell Pendant

It is usually quite easy to find some mussel shells on the beach. When you have collected about four undamaged ones, you can make a pendant like this one. You could make a scallop shell version in the same way. The coating of pearl nail varnish hardly shows, but it adds a pretty, extra touch, although the shells look beautiful in themselves.

Materials: 4 mussel shells; 8 large–size jump rings; 100 cm silky knitting yarn; pearl nail lacquer. **Tools, etc.**: 2 pairs of small pliers; glue; newspaper; scissors. (Super Epoxy Adhesive would be most effective for this necklace, but you can use other fairly strong glue, preferably reinforced when dry with Sellotape.)

▶1   Lacquer the shells inside with pearl nail varnish. When·dry, varnish the outside except on the area to be glued, at the top backs.

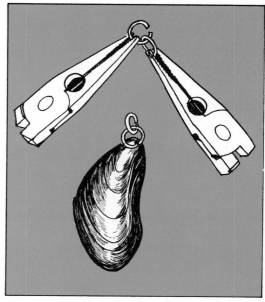

▶2   Use pliers to open a jump ring and slip it through a second ring. Close the jump ring again. Make four pairs of jump rings.

▶3   Glue the jump rings to the top backs of the mussel shells, so that one ring sticks out above each shell.

▶4   When dry, slip the cord through the first mussel-shell jump ring. About 45 cm from one end, tie the mussel shell to the cord. Tie on the other mussel shells in turn a short distance apart.

▶5   Tie the cord ends together. Trim.

Small Things from Shells

When you look for pretty shells at the sea-side on your next visit, you could have fun trying to find matching ones, or unusual kinds to make into jewellery.

Make sure you clean out any snail-shape or spiral shells very thoroughly straightaway, and wash them well so that the bony shape is completely bare inside—if not you might have to deal with a nasty smell later!

Shell Brooches

A particularly fine shell can be easily made into a brooch, like the one shown below.

Materials: beautiful shells; some pink or blue pearl nail lacquer; brooch pins from the rock or craft shop; a small polished stone to glue at the base if a scallop shell is being used, either from the beach or the rock shop. **Tools, etc.**: glue; newspaper; sandpaper.

▶1 Spread newspapers. Lacquer inside the shells with nail varnish. When dry, lacquer the outside, except the glued area. Leave to dry.

▶2 Smear glue on to the brooch fitting, and shell. Press them together and hold until the glue begins to set. Repeat for any other shells.

▶3 Glue the polished stone inside the scallop shell. (Roughen the wrong side of the stone first with sandpaper to make it stick more effectively.)

Shell Headband

Wear this mermaid headband to a party.

Materials: a plastic Alice-band; a few small scallop shells; pale pink pearl nail lacquer. **Tools, etc.**: glue (Super Epoxy Adhesive works well for this); a tape-measure; a pencil; newspaper.

▶1 Lacquer the shells except underneath at the back.

▶2 Measure and mark the centre of the Alice-band, and the position of the other shells, equally spaced apart.

▶3 Arrange the shells in order from the largest at the centre to the smallest at each side.

▶4 Glue the largest shell to the centre mark. Hold it until the glue sets well. Glue on the other shells, one at a time.

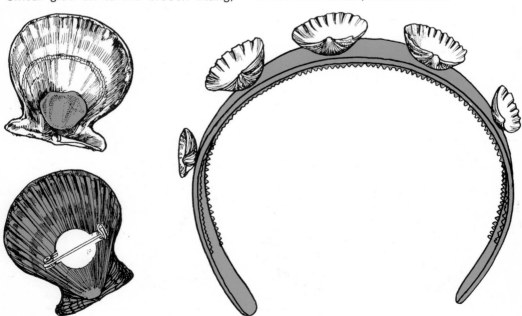

Even the tiniest shells can be used to make perfect ornaments. If you have some, and wonder what to do with them, a visit to the jewellery fittings section of the rock shop will give you plenty of ideas. There you will find, apart from brooch and pendant and bracelet fittings, all sorts of novelties. Cuff-links; key-rings; even metal backs for making buttons.

Shell Buttons

People will hardly believe the buttons you are wearing are a row of real shells.

Materials: 6 small, preferably fancy shells; 6 metal button shank attachments. **Tools, etc.**: glue.

▶1 Spread glue on the back of the shells, and on to each button attachment.

▶2 Press them together, and hold until the glue is slightly set.

Shell Hairslide

Hair ornaments can be jewelled too, and why not with some of nature's own jewels: little shells?

Materials: a hairslide; a row of small matching shells; pink pearl nail lacquer. **Tools, etc.**: glue.

▶1 Spread glue evenly along the hairslide.

▶2 Press the shells into the glue side by side, or overlapping slightly if the right shape.

▶3 When the glue has dried, lacquer the shells pale, pearly pink.

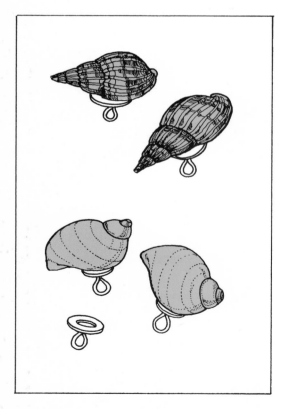

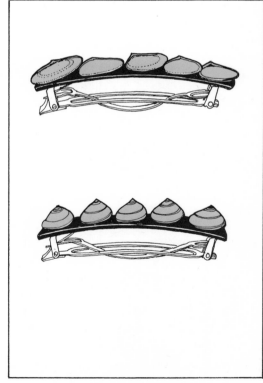

Shell Comb

A curved comb with gold or silver painted shells glued along the top could be a party piece.

Materials: a curved comb; some tiny shells; silver, gold or other coloured paint, or pearl nail lacquer. **Tools, etc.**: glue; tissue paper; newspaper.

▶1 Spread out newspaper. Glue some shells—arranged in a design if you wish—along the curved top of the comb.

▶2 Place the comb on newspaper and cover the teeth with tissue paper.

▶3 Spray the shells, silver, or gold, or any other colour.

▶4 When the paint is dry, move the paper protecting the comb teeth, and you have another attractive hair ornament.

Shell Earrings

If you have been lucky enough to find some matching shells like these, you could make them into earrings.

Materials: 2 matching shells; 2 screw fastening metal earring attachments (or fittings for pierced ears, if you prefer), 2 large bell caps from the rock shop; pearl nail lacquer. **Tools, etc.**: glue; pliers; sandpaper; Plasticine; newspaper.

▶1 Lacquer the shells with nail varnish and leave them to dry.

▶2 Roll out and flatten the Plasticine. Stand the shells point down in it.

▶3 Spread glue on the tops of the shells and inside the bell cap. Press the bell caps on to the shells. Leave to dry.

▶4 When the glue has set hard, hook the open loop in the earring fastening through the bell cap loop. Close the loop with pliers.

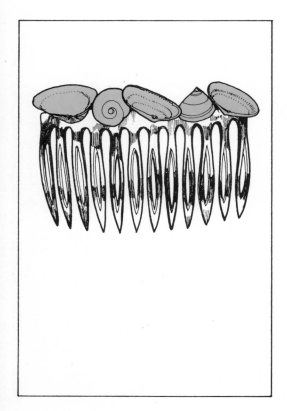

Shell and Acorn Cup Jewels

Picture-Wire Bracelet

Wire is good for making into jewellery. It can be twisted into diamond, square or coil shapes, or made into links or chains. You can thread beads on wire or, as here, glue a shell or small stone to the coil.

It is important to make sure that any sharp or rough ends are sealed or twisted back and covered, so that they won't scratch!

Materials: gold picture-wire no. 2 gauge; a small shell; some acorn cups painted gold or in another colour; a medium-size cocoa tin, borrowed from the kitchen, for shaping the bracelet, and a lipstick case for shaping the ring. **Tools, etc**.: pliers; wire-cutters; glue; Sellotape; newspaper.

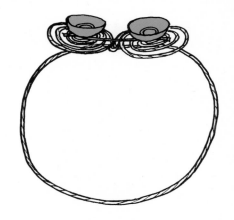

▶1 Cut about 30 cm wire, measuring the length and marking it with a piece of Sello-tape. Snip through the wire using the wire-cutters.

▶2 Remove the Sellotape marker, twist the fraying wire ends, then dip them in glue. Leave to dry.

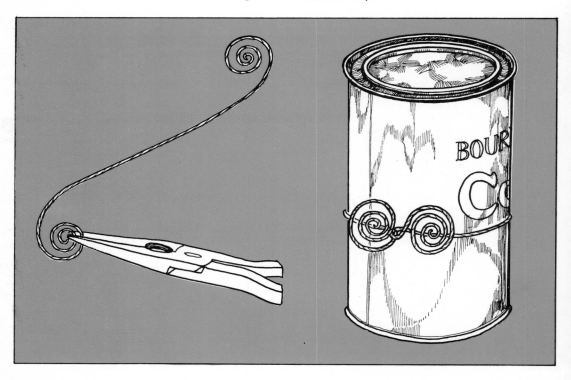

38

▶3 When dry, take one end of the wire and turn it round in a tiny circle, then turn another circle round the first. Continue to coil the wire, until you have a flat coil about 1.5 cm to 2 cm across.

Make another coil at the other end of the wire, but going in the opposite direction.

▶4 Wind the rest of the wire round the cocoa tin, and twist the coils round one another, pressing them flat against the tin at the same time.

▶5 Slide the bracelet off the tin, and slip it over your wrist for size. It can be made smaller by enlarging the coils, if you wish, or unwound a little for a larger size.

▶6 Glue the painted acorn cups on to the centre of the coils.

Picture-Wire Ring

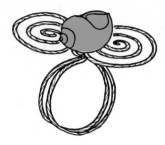

▶1 Measure and cut about 20 cm picture-wire, as you did when making the bracelet. Dip the wire ends in glue.

▶2 When dry, wind tiny coils at each end of the wire, as for the bracelet, to about 1 cm across.

▶3 Wind the wire twice round the lipstick case and twist the coils together.

▶4 Slide the ring off the lipstick, and try on for size. If it is too tight, unwind it a little; if too loose, twist it further.

▶5 Glue the shell to the centre of the coils.

▶6 Lacquer the shell with nail varnish, avoiding the glue because nail varnish will soften some types of adhesive.

Plastic Resin Shell Pendant

You may have seen transparent plastic pendants or paperweights with things like flowers or clockwork parts floating inside them. They are quite easy to make and perfect for nature jewellery. Plants or stones or shells can look really amazing trapped inside what looks like a block of glass.

You could use a plastic embedding kit which contains everything you need to begin the hobby, or buy the essential materials and tools individually from the list below, and find your own moulds. Release wax is needed for ceramic moulds.

Materials: a bottle of plastic resin and a bottle of plastic resin hardener (from a craft or art materials shop, or some toy shops); a sea-horse, crab shell, everlasting flower or any other suitably sized natural object; 50 cm gold-coloured picture-wire no. 2 gauge; 90 cm gilt chain and 2 metal tag ends (from a rock or craft shop). **Tools, etc.**: a millilitre measuring beaker; an orange stick (the sort used for manicuring nails) or similar stick; a polythene round-shaped mould or plastic carton approx. 6 cm across × 1.5 cm deep; a pair of small pliers; paper tissue or kitchen roll; rubber gloves; newspaper.

There are some important safety rules to observe when working with plastic resin, so if you decide to try this craft do take care to follow them:

A. Wear well-fitting gloves while you work. If any resin or hardener gets on you or your clothes, wash it off at once.

Wipe up any spills straightaway with paper tissue or a piece of kitchen roll. ALWAYS throw these in the dustbin, NEVER in the fire.

B. Because resin and hardener are inflammable, be sure not to use them anywhere near a flame or fire.

C. Always work with the door open because the resin gives off a strong chemical smell, and ventilate your room well.

▶1 Your block of resin is made in three stages. First coat a ceramic mould, if used, with release wax as directed. You don't need this if you are using a polythene or plastic mould.

Measure the resin out carefully following the directions given in the instruction leaflet or on the bottle, and add the plastic resin hardener, also as directed, drop by drop to the resin. Stir these two substances together with the orange stick. When poured into the mould, they will in time solidify.

▶2 When this has hardened, the shell or stone to be embedded is laid on top, and covered with another layer of resin, mixed according to directions. (The proportions for resin and hardener are not always the same for each stage.)

▶3 When the second layer has hardened, a third layer is poured on top.

The complete block of plastic will take a day or two to harden. When it has done so, turn it out like a jelly from a mould (although it will not quiver!) and you will see the object firmly embedded in the middle. Lots of layers of resin can be used if you wish to scatter items in the piece of jewellery.

▶4 Now that you are ready to make your shell pendant, cover the table with newspaper. Bend the picture-wire in half and place the folded part under the pendant.

Bind the picture-wire tightly round the side of the plastic cast and twist the wires together in a rope at the top.

▶5. Pass the ends of the wire through the ends of the chain and twist the wire ends round the wire again at each side, to fasten them.

Slip the open sides of the tag ends over the rough ends of the twisted wire, to prevent them from scratching you when wearing the pendant. Close the tag ends firmly with pliers.

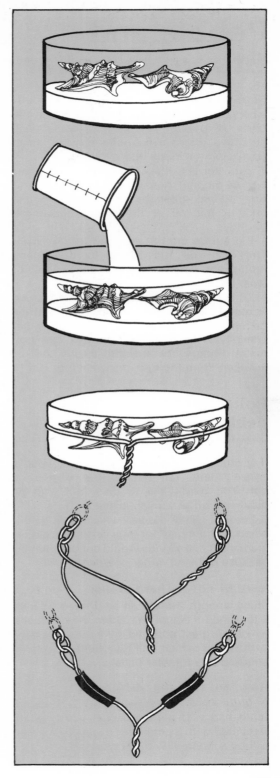

Pebble and Stone Jewellery

Stones and little pebbles make lovely, hard-wearing jewellery. Next time you are on the beach or by a stream look for some small attractive ones; even quite tiny grit-sized stones can be made into mosaics.

You can see the colours of the pebbles best by dipping them in water, and watching how the red, green, brown, black and white rock or mineral of the stones shows up brightly.

Big stones are not so good for jewellery. They can be too heavy for the metal fittings and could even be uncomfortable to wear because of their weight.

You can either mount the stones on home-made fittings of wood, cork, buttons or stiff cardboard, etc., with safety-pin fastenings for brooches; or you can buy metal fittings for making every sort of jewellery from the rock or craft shop.

Polishing and varnishing pebbles and stones

If a stone is a good colour and shape, it doesn't matter too much if it is polished or not. You might like to give it a coat of picture or other varnish instead.

Smooth, hard stones which look shiny when wet are best for jewellery. The sandy, muddy or chalky kinds would not be suitable, because of being rather powdery.

Hard or not-so-hard stones

Shiny smooth stones can be divided up into two broad categories: *quite hard stones* which are best polished by hand, and *very hard stones* which will give better results if polished in a tumbler polisher.

How to tell the difference:

A *quite hard stone* will show a definite score mark with perhaps a chalky line, when scratched with a penknife; a *very hard stone* will be scratched without marking.

Grinding materials

As stone is hard material, the grits used to smooth it have to be even harder. You need special black glittery powder called silicon carbide bought from a rock shop. When this is rubbed over the surface of a suitable stone for a long time, either by hand or in a tumbler polisher, it will smooth the stone and remove any scratches.

Silicon carbide grit comes in various grades, ranging from coarse and gritty sizes to powdery fine grit. Sometimes it is bonded on a kind of sandpaper called wet and dry silicon carbide paper.

(i) Grinding

HAND POLISHING

With silicon carbide grit:

First mix the coarse grit into a paste with water in a tough glass bowl, or on a piece of plate-glass, and rub the stone round and

round, and over and over in it. When the stone is smooth enough, every bit of the grit should be washed away in a bucket, Next the stone is rubbed with medium grit. This has to be cleaned away too before the stone is rubbed over with really fine grit. Use kitchen paper towel for wiping any receptacles, and throw it away, because the coarse grits *must* be kept completely separate from the finer grits.

With wet and dry silicon carbide paper:

This is a cleaner, easier way to work, because you won't have the problem of the different-sized grit particles getting mixed up with one another. The paper is used wet, and rubbed over the stone, working from the coarse grade through a medium stage to the finest grade.

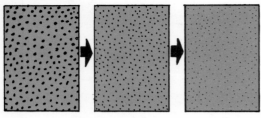

Hand polishing is quite a slow job, but if you do it patiently, in the end you will have a smooth, scratch-free stone with a beautiful glossy surface.

TUMBLER POLISHING

In case you have never seen a tumbler polisher, this is a little machine which turns a barrel full of pebbles over and over so that they rub together and wear one another smooth. Water and the correct amount of grit have to be added to the stones when the barrel is loaded.

The routine for tumbler polishing is the same as for hand polishing with coarse, medium and fine grinds, though the job can sometimes be completed by the machine in only two grinds.

The tumbler polisher always comes with complete directions for polishing stones, for you to refer to.

Cleaning up in between stages is important whichever way you work.

Be prepared for a long job even if you are lucky enough to possess a tumbler polisher. The grinding and polishing process takes about three weeks night and day from start to finish.

(ii) Polishing the stones

The polishing process is done at the end, quite separately, after every trace of grit has been cleared away. The polish used is usually a powder called cerium oxide or tin oxide.

If you are using a tumbler polisher, the powder has to be added to a barrel reserved exclusively for polishing.

If you are polishing by hand, the powder should be mixed to a thick paste with water; the polisher can be a brush-back with white felt stretched tightly over the wood.

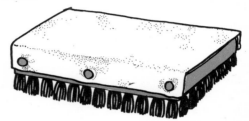

Polish the stone as though you are polishing a pair of shoes, as hard as you can until it becomes glossy. Then you can stop work, thankfully, and clear up.

Finding out about stones

There are several ways of learning all about pebbles and stones. One is to go as often as possible to look at the collections in the Geological Museum in Exhibition Road, London SW7, or to the Mineralogy Department at the Natural History Museum nearby in Cromwell Road.

Your local museum may have a collection of local rocks and minerals too.

Your library is sure to have some books on geology. Another way of finding out about stones imported for making jewellery is to study the catalogue from a rock shop, and if possible visit one to look at the dishes of polished and rough stones there. You may even like to buy a specimen of each kind over a period, and form your own collection with bought stones as well as those that you find yourself.

Jewellery with Home-Made Settings

You can use lids and corks and buttons, and all sorts of other items from around the house, as settings for stones.

Here are a few ideas to set you thinking of the many possibilities.

Stones in the Sand Pendant

You would never believe this elegant piece of jewellery, with two bright red polished stones glued in a sand background, is made out of a cocoa tin lid and string.

Materials: 2 flat stones (we used polished red jasper and a carnelian from the rock shop); a spoonful of sand; a cocoa tin or other lid; coloured or plain string; a brass curtain ring. **Tools, etc.**: glue; sandpaper, or wet and dry silicon carbide paper; Sellotape; newspaper.

▶1   Rub the stones on the wrong side with sandpaper or wet and dry paper, to roughen them.

▶2   Glue the brass curtain ring on the back of the tin so that it sticks up over the edge.

▶3   When the glue is dry, smear some more inside the rim on the front of the lid.

▶4   Press the stones in the middle and shake sand over the glue (and the stones—it will dust off).

▶5   Reinforce the ring with Sellotape.

▶6   Cut 2 lengths of string each 100 cm. Tie them together with a knot at 5 cm intervals.

▶7   Slip the string through the ring on the pendant and tie a knot. Join the ends together with another knot.

Cork and Stones Pendant

Here pale green stones, amazonite, aventurine and bloodstone bought ready polished from the rock shop, have been glued to pieces of cork. (You could use suitable stones picked up on the beach instead.)

Materials: a champagne-type wine bottle cork; 3 polished flat stones; coloured or plain string; 3 brass curtain rings. **Tools, etc.**: mini-hacksaw and board; glue; Sellotape; scissors; sandpaper, or wet and dry silicon carbide paper; newspaper.

▶1 Spread out newspaper. Saw the cork through from top to bottom into three pieces.

▶2 Glue a brass curtain ring on the back of each piece of cork, so that it sticks up over the top edge. Leave to dry.

▶3 Roughen the flat sides of the stones with sandpaper or wet and dry paper.

▶4 Cut 3 lengths of string each 100 cm. Tie them together at one end. Plait them neatly all the way along, and tie a knot at the other end.

▶5 Spread glue on the roughened sides of the stones and on the front of the corks. Press the stones on to the glue and hold them firm. When slightly set, leave them to dry.

▶6 Slot the string through the centre cork ring, and find the string centre. Tie a knot at the ring, and another 4 cm above.

▶7 Tie the other corks at either side.

▶8 Tie the string ends together to form a tassel.

▶9 Reinforce the curtain rings with strips of Sellotape if necessary.

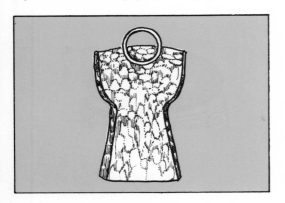

Jewellery with Bought Settings

Even if you have found and polished your own stones and small pebbles to make into jewellery, you may decide you would like to use some of the jewellery fittings we have mentioned, instead of always making your own.

If you live a long way from the nearest rock shop, you can often send to one for a mail order catalogue. In this you will usually find drawings or photographs of all the jewellery fittings available, as well as lists and pictures of stones that are imported from other countries. Tumbler polishers and other equipment can be bought in this way too.

Here are a few simple items you can make using inexpensive metal jewellery fittings.

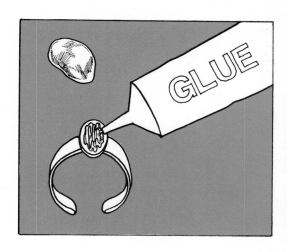

▶2 Smear glue on the back of the stone and on the ring blank.

▶3 Press the pebble and ring together. Hold them until the glue begins to set, then leave to dry.

A larger pebble can be fixed to a brooch setting, or a special polished stone from the rock shop can be glued to a tie-pin in the same way.

Pebble Ring

Materials: a ring fitting (called a ring blank); a small polished or varnished pebble.
Tools, etc.: sandpaper, or wet and dry silicon carbide paper; glue; newspaper.

▶1 Choose which is the prettiest side of the pebble. Rub the other side with wet and dry paper or sandpaper.

A Bracelet of Polished and Unpolished Beach Stones

The bracelet on the opposite page is made with the most common pebbles and pieces of shingle, some unpolished, and yet they look extremely elegant and beautiful made into jewellery.

Materials: a bought bracelet fitting with flat metal shapes joined by jump rings (called a pad fitting); a stone for each pad, chosen to match the others for size. **Tools, etc.**: glue, sandpaper or wet and dry silicon carbide paper; tweezers if available; newspaper.

▶1 Cover the table with newspaper. Lay out the bracelet fitting, and stones. Decide on the arrangement of the stones and place the prettiest sides uppermost. Two of the little round pebbles on our bracelet are polished flint; two are unpolished irregular shapes of beach shingle; the others are polished red carnelians.

▶2 Roughen the surface to be glued with sandpaper or wet and dry paper.

▶3 Spread glue on the first bracelet pad and on the roughened side of the first stone. Press the two together.

▶4 Do the same in turn to all the other stones. Do not move the bracelet until the glue has set.

Here are some good ideas for a present for a man, which look smart and would be useful too!

Polished Flint Cuff-Links

Materials: a pair of bought cuff-link fittings with flat, pad tops; small polished beach flints (or other stones) about 1 cm across. **Tools, etc.**: glue, sandpaper, or wet and dry silicon carbide paper; tweezers if available; newspaper; Plasticine.

▶1 Cover the table with newspaper. Choose the flat side of the flints and rub them with sandpaper or wet and dry paper.

▶2 Press the ends of the cuff-link fittings into the Plasticine, so that the flat, pad ends are on top.

▶3 Spread glue on the cuff-link pads and on the roughened area of the flints. Press the stones on to the cuff-links. Leave for the glue to dry.

Pebble Tie-Pin

Materials: a bought tie-pin fitting; a beautiful flat stone (ours is smoky quartz, a glass-like pale grey stone). **Tools, etc.**: glue; sandpaper, or wet and dry silicon carbide paper; tweezers if available; newspaper.

▶1 Cover the table with newspaper. Roughen the centre of the flattest part of the stone with sandpaper or wet and dry silicon carbide paper.

▶2 Spread glue on the centre of the tie-pin fitting and on the roughened part of the stone. Press them together. Hold for a moment for the glue to dry, then leave to set.

Mosaic Brooch

Materials: a number of stone chips or small polished stones; a quite large brooch fitting, about 3 cm to 4 cm across (or you can use a piece of cardboard for the base with a safety-pin fastening). **Tools, etc.**: tweezers to pick up the stones and place them in position; glue; sandpaper or wet and dry silicon carbide paper; Plasticine; a piece of paper and a pencil; newspaper.

▶1 Design the mosaic. Draw round the brooch fitting, and fill it in with your design drawing. Or you can draw the brooch shape and then arrange the stones on it with tweezers, until you have a pattern to your liking.

Sometimes the prettiest stones you find are the smallest—mere chips. A good way of using them is to glue them on to a background of wood or cardboard to form a mosaic, which is a pattern of small stones. (Glass and other materials are also used for mosaics.)

A metal background is equally suitable. The mosaic brooch shown here is made of extra-small polished pieces of stone glued on a large, round brooch fitting. You can often buy a bag of polished chippings of gemstones fairly inexpensively from the rock shop. The stones come in all the shades of the rainbow.

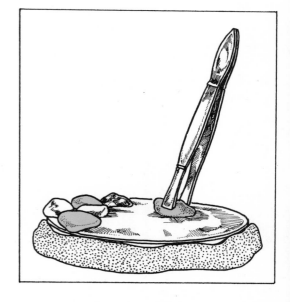

The browns and blacks and whites of grit make decorative designs too; you can even form a picture with them.

So never despise those little gravel pieces you find in the sand or between the pebbles on the beach. They might be just what you are looking for.

▶2 Press the pin side of the brooch fitting into the Plasticine to keep it level.

▶3 Cover the flat area with glue.

▶4 Roughen the sides of the stones to be glued, and place them, one at a time, on the brooch with tweezers. Leave them to dry.